CW00368929

First published in Great Britain in 1996 by Brockhampton Press, a member of the Hodder Headline Group, 20 Bloomsbury Street, London WC1B 3QA.

This series of little gift books was made by Frances Banfield, Kate Brown, Laurel Clark, Penny Clarke, Clive Collins, Melanie Cumming, Nick Diggory, Deborah Gill, David Goodman, Douglas Hall, Maureen Hill, Nick Hutchison, John Hybert, Kate Hybert, Douglas Ingram, Simon London, Patrick McCreeth, Morse Modaberi, Tara Neill, Anne Newman, Grant Oliver, Michelle Rogers, Nigel Soper, Karen Sullivan and Nick Wells.

ISBN 1 86019 443 5

A copy of the CIP data is available from the British Library upon request.

Produced for Brockhampton Press by Flame Tree Publishing, a part of The Foundry Creative Media Company Limited, The Long House, Antrobus Road, Chiswick W4 5HY.

Printed and bound in Italy by L.E.G.O. Spa.

Just For You

FATHER

Illustrated by

Douglas Hall

A.R.C.A.

Selected by Anne Rose

Honour thy father and thy mother, that thy days may be long in the land which the Lord thy God giveth thee.

Exodus, XX:13 (The Fifth Commandment)

A child enters your home and for the next twenty years makes so much noise you can hardly stand it. The child departs, leaving the house so silent you think you are going mad.

John Andrew Holmes

Daddies take you out for trips to their work. My daddy takes me birdwatching. I like my daddy because he tells me stories about when he was a little boy before I go to sleep.

Hannah, 4

There are no stories quite like the very first
Dad stories.
H. Dalton

I took my father for granted,
never thought him courageous.
A clean watchful man
who never raised his voice,
never stood at a barricade
but quietly held his course.
Never unjust to the young,
never betrayed his trust.
Secret in his love.
Now I know the small disciples of day by day
spoke for a valiant heart.
Harry Chapin

Becoming a father is easy enough.
But being one can be rough.
Wilhelm Busch

You can learn many things from children.
How much patience you have, for instance.
Franklin P. Jones

◈

Being a father
Is quite a bother,
But I like it, rather.
Ogden Nash, *Soliloquy in Circles*

◈

Father, dear father, come home with me now,
The clock in the steeple strikes one.
Henry Clay Work, *Come Home, Father*

◈

Directly after God in heaven comes Papa.
Wolfgang Amadeus Mozart

Of all nature's gifts
to the human race,
what is sweeter to a
man than his
children?
Cicero

It is impossible to please all the world and also
one's father.
Jean de la Fontaine, *Fables*

'You are old, Father William,'
the young man said,
'And your hair has become very white,
And yet you incessantly stand on your head —
Do you think, at your age, it is right?'
'In my youth,' Father William replied to his son,
'I feared it might injure the brain;
But now that I'm perfectly sure I have none,
Why, I do it again and again.'
Lewis Carroll, *Alice's Adventures in Wonderland*

The father who holds the baby only when it is
sweet and fresh; who plays on the nursery floor
when things go along like a song; who gingerly
tiptoes away at times of tears or disciplinary show-
downs, is just a dilettante papa, with a touch of
the coward, and not a complete father.
Samuel S. Drury, *Fathers & Sons*

Children are a great comfort in your old age.
They help you reach it faster, too.
Lionel Kaufman

Insanity is hereditary: you can get it from
your children.
Sam Levenson

It is easier for a father to have children than for
children to have a real father.
Pope John XXIII

When I was a boy of fourteen, my father was so ignorant I could hardly stand to have the old man around. But when I got to be twenty-one, I was astounded at how much the old man had learned in seven years.
Mark Twain

The people to whom we owe the most never remind us of our debts. They send no bills ... why do I write this? Because I am thinking of one of the greatest of my own debts — the one to my father.
Edgar A. Guest, *Moments with Father*

There are times when parenthood seems nothing
but feeding the mouth that bites you.
Peter de Vries

⧈

My father would pick me up and hold me high in
the air. He dominated my life as long as he lived,
and was the love of my life for many years after
he died.
Eleanor Roosevelt

⧈

Wife, the Athenians rule the Greeks, and I rule
the Athenians, and thou me, and our son, thee; let
him then use sparingly the authority which makes
him, foolish as he is, the most powerful person in
Greece.
Themistocles

We had great fun and a real sense of
accomplishment as small kids. Thank you, Dad.
Katharine Hepburn

A little child, a limber elf singing, dancing
to itself ...
Make such a vision to the sight, as fills a father's
eyes with light.
Samuel Taylor Coleridge

Children begin by loving their parents. After a
time they judge them. Rarely, if ever, do they
forgive them.
Oscar Wilde, *A Woman of No Importance*

No man can possibly know what life means, what the world means, what anything means, until he has a child and loves it. And then the whole universe changes and nothing will ever seem exactly as it seemed before.

Lafcadio Hearn

... Her young, handsome, rich, petty father seemed to be the only relation she had in the world. They had always played together and been fond of each other.

Frances Hodgson Burnett, *A Little Princess*

If the man who turnips cries,
Cry not when his father dies,
'Tis proof that he had rather
Have a turnip than his father.

Dr Samuel Johnson

He that will have his son have a respect for him and his orders, must himself have a greater reverence for his son.

John Locke, *Some Thoughts Concerning Education*

Father is rather vulgar, my dear. The word Papa, besides, gives a pretty form to the lips.
Charles Dickens, *Little Dorrit*

When a father sets out to teach his little son to walk, he stands in front of him and holds his two hands on either side of the child, so that he cannot fall, and the boy goes toward his father between his father's hands. But the moment he is close to his father, he moves away a little and holds his hands further apart, so that the child may learn to walk.
The Baal Shem Tov

It is a wise father that knows his own child.
William Shakespeare, *The Merchant of Venice*

As we read the school reports upon our children, we realize with a sense of relief that can rise to delight that thank Heavens — nobody is reporting in this fashion upon us.

J. B. Priestley

A man is so in the way in the house.

Mrs Gaskell, *Cranford*

Last night my child was born ... If you ever become a father, I think the strangest and strongest sensation of your life will be hearing for the first time the thin cry of your own child ... it is a very tender, but also a very ghostly feeling.

Lafcadio Hearn

Full fathom five thy father lies;
Of his bones are coral made:
Those are pearls that were his eyes;
Nothing of him that doth fade,
But doth suffer a sea-change
Into something rich and strange.
William Shakespeare, *The Tempest*

The fact that boys are allowed to exist at all is evidence of a remarkable Christian forbearance among men.

Ambrose Bierce

The parent who could see his boy as he really is, would shake his head and say: 'Willie is no good: I'll sell him.'

Stephen Leacock, *The Lot of the Schoolmaster*

The fathers have eaten sour grapes, and the children's teeth are set on edge.

Ezekiel, XVIII:2

She liked to think of that. To keep the house for her father; to ride with him and sit at the head of his table when he had dinner-parties; to talk to him and read his books — that would be what she would like most in the world.

Frances Hodgson Burnett, *A Little Princess*

I could not point to any need in childhood as
strong as that for a father's protection.
Sigmund Freud

Children are a poor man's riches.
Thomas Fuller

The words that a father speaks to his children in
the privacy of home are not heard
by the world, but, as in
whispering galleries,
they are clearly heard
at the end and by
posterity.
Jean Paul Richter

Let no one who loves be called altogether
unhappy. Even love unreturned has its rainbow.
J. M. Barrie, *The Little Minister*

The child is the father of the man.
William Wordsworth

My daddy goes to work and gets money.
Hayley, 5

He that loves not his wife and children, feeds a
lioness at home and broods a nest of sorrows.
Jeremy Taylor, *Sermon*

... the poorest poor
Long for some moments in a weary life
When they can know and feel that they have been
Themselves the fathers and the dealers out
Of some small blessings.
Wordsworth, *The Old Cumberland Beggar*

I recently turned fifty, which is young for a tree,
mid-life for an elephant and ancient for a quarter-
miler, whose son now says, Dad, I just can't run
the quarter with you any more unless I bring
something to read.
Bill Cosby, *Time Flies*

It is the family's expectation that will make father
into his best, and biggest self.
Samuel S. Drury, *Fathers & Sons*

Fatherhood is...
pretending that the present you love most is
soap-on-a-rope.
Bill Cosby

You are a king by your own fireside, as much as
any monarch on his throne.
Miguel de Cervantes

Grown-ups never understand anything for
themselves, and it is tiresome for children to be
always and forever explaining things to them.
Antoine de Saint-Exupéry, *The Little Prince*

When a father gives to his son, both laugh; when
a son gives to his father, both cry.
Yiddish proverb

The one thing father always gave up in Lent was going to church.
Clarence Day, *My Father's Dark Hour*

Papa never climbed Everest or made the 'Guinness Book of World Records'. He never read the classics or saw an original painting by Braque ... I was aware that years of having known and loved my father have transformed him from Pap, the simple human being, into Papa, the near saint. And I have come to the conclusion that there is nothing wrong with that.
Leo Buscaglia, *Papa, My Father*

My father had a profound influence over me — he was a lunatic.
Spike Milligan

My father could never have run a filling station. Giving free air, or even directions, would have left him apoplectic.

Richard Armour, *Pills, Potions — and Granny*

My father is in a bad mood. This means he is feeling better.

Sue Townsend, *The Secret Diary of Adrian Mole*

Like father like son.

Proverb

The human heart, at whatever age, opens only to the heart that opens in return.

Maria Edgeworth

No man is responsible for his father.
That is entirely his mother's affair.
Margaret Turnball

The thing that impresses me most about America
is the way parents obey their children.
Edward, Duke of Windsor

Children pick up
words as pigeons peas,
And utter them again as
God shall please.
Old English proverb

To love is to admire with
the heart; to admire is to
love with the mind.
Théophile Gautier

Govern a small family as you would cook a small
fish, very gently.
Chinese proverb

Govern a small family as you would cook a small
fish, very gently.
Chinese proverb

What the children hear at home soon flies abroad.
Henry Beecher Ward

Advice is a stranger, if welcome he stays for the
night; if not welcome he returns the same day.
Malagasy proverb

Blessed be childhood, which brings down
something of heaven into the midst of our rough
earthliness.
Henri Frederick Amiel

A man who prides himself on his ancestry is
like the potato plant, the best part of which
is underground.
Spanish proverb

I don't call my father father, I call him Daddy.
Isabel, 7

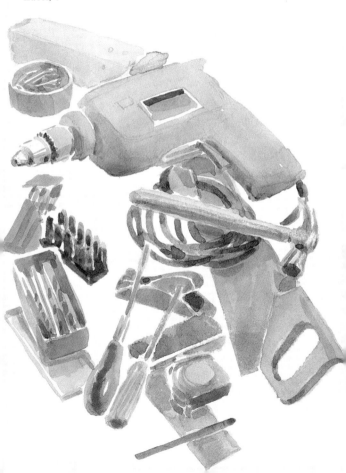

I know fame and power are for the birds. But then suddenly life comes into focus for me. And, ah, there stand my kids. I love them.

Lee Iacocca

My father goes to work on the train.
And has fun.

Bella, 7

Children's children are the crown of old men;
And the glory of children are their fathers.

Proverbs, XVII:6

But her father smiled on the fairest child
He ever held in his arms.
Emily Brontë, *A Day Dream*

⊡

To be a successful father ... there's one absolute
rule: when you have a kid, don't look at it for the
first two years.
Ernest Hemingway, *Papa Hemingway*

⊡

The presence of my children affects me with deep
weariness and depression. I do not see them until
luncheon, as I have my breakfast alone in the
library, and they are in fact well trained to avoid
my part of the house but I am aware of them from
the moment I wake ...
Evelyn Waugh

Unless he happens to work for Halston, the
American father cannot be trusted to put together
combinations of clothes. He is a man who was
taught that the height of fashion was to wear two
shoes that matched; and so, children can easily
convince him of the elegance of whatever they do
or don't want to wear.
Bill Cosby, *Fatherhood*

Better to be driven out from among men than to
be disliked of children.
Richard Henry Dana, *The Idle Man: Domestic Life*

The childhood shows the man
As morning shows the day.
John Milton, *Paradise Regained*

Parents are the bones upon which children sharpen their teeth.

Peter Ustinov, *Dear Me*

If you have never been hated by your child, you have never been a parent.

Bette Davis

I used to tell a joke about the shame we suffered in Glasgow because he was a teetotaller, and the disgrace on Saturday nights of him being thrown into pubs.

Arnold Brown, *No Accounting for Comedy*

My father was the only person I ever knew who
addressed babies in their prams as if they were his
contemporaries. He spoke as he would to a bank
manager or a bishop: friendly but respectful.
Joyce Grenfell, *George - Don't Do That*

Dad, Dad, when you come up to give
us a bit of real trouble, can you bring
us up a drink of water as well?
Michael Rosen, *These Two Children*

49

A fool despiseth his father's correction;
But he that regardeth reproof is prudent.
Proverbs, XV:5

I love my dad because when I'm bigger we will
have a dog and he means it.
Adam, 5

I sometimes wished he would realize that he was
poor instead of being that most nerve-racking of
phenomena, a rich man without money.
Peter Ustinov, *Dear Me*

A man's father is his king.
Pirke de Rabbi Eliezer

The joys of parents are secret and so are their griefs and fears.

Francis Bacon, *Essays: Of Parents and Children*

I suppose that the high-water mark of my youth in Columbus, Ohio, was the night the bed fell on my father.

James Thurber, *My Life and Hard Times*

You are old Father William, the young man cried,
The few looks which are left you are grey;
You are hale, Father William, a hearty old man,
Now tell me the reason, I pray.

Robert Southey,
The Old Man's Comforts, and How He Gained Them

My heart belongs to daddy.

Cole Porter

＊

The fundamental defect of fathers, in our
competitive society, is that they want their
children to be a credit to them.

Bertrand Russell, *Sceptical Essays*

＊

You may go into the fields or down the lane, but
don't go into Mr McGregor's garden: your Father
had an accident there; he was put in a pie by
Mrs McGregor.

Beatrix Potter, *The Tale of Peter Rabbit*

My Dad is brilliant ...
It's great to have a dad like mine. It's brilliant.
Nick Butterworth, *My Dad is Brilliant*

The law of heredity is that all undesirable traits
come from the other parent.
Anonymous

My father is nice.
He is strong.
I like my father.
Tom, 6

It's a wonderful feeling when your father becomes not a god but a man to you — when he comes down from the mountain and you see he's this man with weaknesses. And you love him as this whole being, not just as a figurehead.
Robin Williams

Children sweeten labours, but they make misfortunes more bitter.
Francis Bacon, *Essays: Of Parents and Children*

Children suck the mother
when they are young, and
the father when they are
grown.
English proverb

She didn't love her father -
she idolized him. He was the one great
love in her life. No other man ever
measured up to him.
Mary S. Lovell

A dad is a man haunted by death, fears, anxieties,
But who seems to his children the haven from all
harm. And who makes them certain that whatever
happens — it will all come right.
Clara Ortega

Now Tom would be a driver and Maria go to sea,
And my papa's a banker and as rich as he can be;
Robert Louis Stevenson, *The Lamplighter*

I was not close to my father, but he was very special to me. Whenever I did something as a little girl — learn to swim or act in a school play, for instance — he was fabulous. There would be this certain look in his eyes. It made me feel great.

Diane Keaton

Ask your father and he will tell you.
Deuteronomy, XXXII:7

I gave Dad a very special picture which I painted
at play-group.
And he gave me a ride on his shoulders most of
the way home.
Shirley Hughes, *Giving*

Daddy is delicious
Daddy is kind
Daddy is so wonderful
Because he is all mine
Frances, 9

A man that is young in years, may be old in
hours, if he have lost no time. But that
happeneth rarely.
Francis Bacon, *Essays*

Acknowledgements:

The Publishers wish to thank everyone who gave permission to reproduce the quotes in this book. Every effort has been made to contact the copyright holders, but in the event that an oversight has occurred, the publishers would be delighted to rectify any omissions in future editions of this book. Children's quotes printed courtesy of Herne Hill School, Hannah Rough and Kingfisher County Primary School; Auberon Waugh and Evelyn Waugh, from *Will This Do?* reprinted courtesy of Random House; *Papa My Father*, Leo F. Buscaglia, SLACK Inc.; *Fatherhood, Time Flies,* Bill Cosby, reprinted courtesy of Bantam Books, Transworld Publishers; *Soliloquy in Circles*, from *Verses from 1929 on*, Ogden Nash, reprinted courtesy of Curtis Brown Ltd., *The Haunt of Time*, Harry Chapin © 1981 William L. Bauhan, Publisher, Dublin, N.H., *Moments with Father*, Edgar A. Guest, reprinted courtesy of Hallmark; Robin Williams in *Rolling Stone*, 1988, published by Straight Arrow Publishers Inc., New York; *The Secret Diary of Adrian Mole*, Sue Townsend, published by Methuen Children's Books; Michael Rosen, published by John Murray (Publishers) Limited; *My Dad is Brilliant*, Nick Butterworth, published by HarperCollins; *The Tale of Peter Rabbit*, Beatrix Potter, published by Frederick Warne, a division of Viking Penguin; *Giving*, Shirley Hughes, published by Bodley Head, a division of Random House UK.